Ba Bii Dwe We Win
Sounds of Living

Poems by *Migizikwe Nindizhikaaz*
Mildred "Tinker" Schuman

Ba Bii Dwe We Win: **Sounds of Living**

Copyright 2021 by *Migizikwe Nindizhikaaz*, Mildred "Tinker" Schuman. All rights reserved. Except for short excerpts for review purposes, no part of this book may be reproduced or transmitted in any form without the written permission of the author.

Published by: Eagle Woman Publishing
                    15524 Indian Village Rd.
                    Lac du Flambeau, WI 54538
                    E-mail: tinkerschuman13@gmail.com

Cover Art: Weaving by Mary Burns, inspired in part by a photo by Anne Laure Camilleri
Book and Cover Design: Lora Hagen

Schuman, Mildred "Tinker", 1946 -
        Ba Bii Dwe We Win: Sounds of Living
        written by *Migizikwe Nindizhikaaz*, Mildred "Tinker" Schuman
        ISBN 978-0-578-87746-4
Library of Congress Control Number: 2021905628

Printed in the United States

10 9 8 7 6 5 4 3 2 1

Contents

My Dad and His Nature	9
TERESA	10
My Son Wears a Bandana	11
Our Creator	12
Collected Artifacts	13
For Mother	15
Between the Nodes	16
Message from Mother	17
In the Second Beyond Stillness	19
DANCE A NEW LIFE	20
If I Live	21
A TOOL	22
Purify	23
Today My Relatives	24
No Reason To Be Lost	25
EAGLE OF THE MORNING SUNRISE	26
Whey The Great Spirit	27
Handle Gently	28
MY TRIP TO NEENAH	29
NASHAKWA MAKWAKWE– BEAR WOMAN– KATHY BORGENHAGEN	30
NIIYO'GIIZHIGOOKWE–Mary Ellen Baker	32
NO TURNING BACK	33
Madoodooswan–sweatlodge	34
Refreshment To My Soul	35
ANCESTRAL WOMEN OF CREATIVE SPIRIT	36
Happy To Be Alive	37
MINOMANIDOIKWE–Elizabeth Vetterneck	38
EAGLE SPIRIT	40
NOKOMIS DIBIKI GIIZIS – GRANDMOTHER MOON	41
WOMEN OFFERING FLOWERS TO *NIBI* (WATER)	42
NIMAKWA	43
LOOKING OUT ACROSS THE WATER, A SPIRITUAL LINE OF WAVES	44
Substantial Evidence	45
WOMAN	46
Of the Creation	47
SNOW ANGELS ON THE ICE	48
It Is Well With My Soul	49
FOR THE *ANISHINAABE* PEOPLE	50
For Lac du Flambeau Relatives	52
THE BUS RIDE	53
WALK TO THE WOODSTOVE	54
ISHKODE	55
For Priority	56
Looking into the Sun	57
VISIONS OF MEMORIES	58
Sweat Lodge	59
Older Eagle	60
We Are One	61
NIIWIN GAKEYAA	62
Dear	63
MINO BIMAADIZIWIN	64
Precious You	65
Early Morning	66
Big Reservation in the Sky	67
ABOUT THE AUTHOR	69

BA BII DWE WE WIN: SOUNDS OF LIVING
DEDICATED TO MY FATHER JOHN JOSEPH SCHUMAN SR.

JOHN JOSEPH SCHUMAN SR. is the son of Katherine McArthur Schuman and Edward McArthur, Grandson of Sophia Shadamo McAuthur (*BIINDIGINASSONOKWE*—"she who comes in woman"). Sophia was a member of the Lac du Flambeau Lake Superior Band Chippewa/Ojibwe Nation. His Grandfather William McArthur was a nontribal member. They lived on the Trout Lake Island in northern Wisconsin.

From limited information, this is what I understand of my relatives. My great-grandmother Sophia was known as a medicine woman who would help Native American Indians and non-Indian. People went to get healing. Sophia wore long dresses and would walk from Arbor Vitae, Trout Lake, to Lac du Flambeau. My dad, one of her six grandchildren, met my Mother Beatrice Ritchie, and they married January 13, 1934. They had eleven children.

YEARS LATER

My Dad and Mom had their home in Lac du Flambeau, Wisconsin 1010 Peace Pipe Rd., aka Hwy. D. The residence was by Moss Lake, aka Mud Lake. My dad built the house. It had a kitchen with a wooden floor, living room, and three bedrooms. We had an outhouse. My dad put in a well so we had running water. Before that we had to take a wagon and go one block and fill the silver milk bottles. Laundry day we would haul water from the lake.

At the Fourth of July gathering, we had a cookout picnic on the lakeside. My sisters would cook food, my brothers played guitars. We had fun.

My Mother always had family gatherings for the holidays each season. One time, I had to go in the house for some things in the kitchen. My dad was in his bedroom located at the end of the hall. He had a lake view. His room was filled with fishing gear and his hunting guns. He heard my voice in the kitchen and called to me. I went down there. He said, "Tinker, listen." I obliged my Dad's request and quickly paid attention. I stood there and listened. "What did you hear?" my Dad asked. Answering, I could hear my brothers and sisters talking, guitars playing, singing, noises of laughter, children playing games. I could hear the birds, flies, mosquitoes, bees buzzing by the garden, a radio on, television on, kids swimming. My dad said, "These are the sounds of living."

ACKNOWLEDGEMENTS
I AM 75, THANK YOU

I AM HONORING OUR GREAT SPIRIT for direction and making this all possible. Totally a blessing to share through free verse poetry and short stories.

IN HUMBLENESS, *MIIGWECH*, THANK YOU GREAT SPIRIT CREATOR OF HEAVEN AND EARTH.

SPIRITUAL BLESSINGS OF *BA BII DWE WIN*: THE SOUNDS OF LIVING COMING TO LIFE.

COMING THROUGH WORDS, sounds of loving family, friends, relatives. Through ceremonies each day. Creator Surrounds my life daily. I'm astounded and precious for the gift of life.

I am honored and Thank Jesus for your light of Life. You gave your life for all people. Thank you for being part of my healings and protection. Thank you Spirit angels watching over me, helping me.

Thank you to my daughter Teresa Elm Mitchell – *Peko samo kwe* – Sunset woman; her husband Frank Mitchell Sr. – *Benashii* – Bird; and grandchildren *Mino Giizhig* – Good sky, *Mooshkinetakwad* – First sound from Drum, and *Aabita waasaakanebik* – Halfway in the light of Spring.

My Son Robert Elm – *Nakoosa* – Little Star, *Giibwanazi* – Hawk, Anakwad – Cloud, *Mke demko kwe* – Black bear woman, *Biiwaabiko Inini* – Ironman, and *Dabaso Anakwad* – Thunderbird flying under the Cloud.

Thank you for my sister Mary and my sister Maggie and Dave Hume and their families.

Thank you for my great-grandchildren and the future.

Thank you for my friend Frank Cobb.

I wish to acknowledge all my SPONSORS:
Lac du Flambeau Tribal council, Dr. Norman Wetzel, Frank Cobb, Margaret Delafuente, Natalie Andrews, Betsy A. Behnke, Beth Tornes, Michelle Erdman, Dona Yahola, Mark and Michelle Zanoni, Cheryl Boyd, Joe Wildcat, Sr., Katrina Isaacson and Johanna May's Fine Teas, Sister Marla Lang.

I am grateful to Leon Boycee Valliere for translating the title of my book, to Mary Burns and John Bates helping me with their LOVE and Expertise, and to Beth Tornes and Lora Hagen for their help in making this book come to life.

Thank you, *Migizikwe Nindizhikaaz*

My Dad and His Nature

Built a home for his family.
Inside the home was laughter and sometimes pain.
Hard work, he labored most of his life doing road construction work.
My dad, he loved to fish the four seasons, spring, summer, fall, and winter.
He taught me to fish and clean them. Then Dad taught me to drive the boat while fishing on Pokegama Lake by some small islands. Getting too close, I sheared a pin; lucky he had a spare in his fishing tackle box.
Dad would hunt deer, ducks. When he trapped muskrats, he sold the hides.
He taught me to hunt deer. One time November family hunt, I was on watch standing in the cold morning while some hunters were making a drive. There up on the small hill I saw a deer. The deer stopped and moved his head around. I was dressed in hunter red color. I definitely was excited thinking this food would be on the table. I shot and he dropped. It was a spike buck. My brothers took care of him. This was my third year of hunting. Finally!! I got my deer. We were done hunting for the day and celebrated.
My dad let me drive his vehicle after fishing one year. My younger sisters wanted some marshmallows so I drove uptown to the store. Coming back home and turning into the driveway, I knocked a little tree down. 1 didn't turn sharp enough. Got yelled at. Then he said,
I shouldn't have yelled, because I was learning to drive.
My dad said to me, "If you want something, work for it." I had to, we had a big family. Then when I got paid, I had to give half to my Mother.
Thanks Dad.

TERESA

Teresa is my flesh and blood
Created by a will
and not only mine.
Her eyes are the color of cinnamon.
Her hair is the color of woody brown.

My daughter,
Peko samo quay is the Sunset Lady.
Vigorous emotions strike horizons,
Kind and gentle, reminds me of apple pie.
From her growth of a seed to completion.
Each year she ripens to fulfillment
And serves her purpose, not for me
But for herself and for whoever
Engulfs her abundance.

The light surrounds and the birds make music.
WAIT *Nimaamaa*, I'm still youthful
And I will conquer each thought daily.

My Son Wears a Bandana

He is aware
Of his classmates mocking his long hair,
"They call me a girl sometime.
Why can't I cut my hair?"

He is aware
Of innocent prejudices
Taught by primary people
The first nation culture, they
Don't understand.

He is aware
That he is Indian and different from others.
"Be PROUD of who you are.
Grandfather created you! It is his will,
Others show their ignorance first."

He is aware
The teachers asked if he
Could bring his traditional clothing
To school to teach his classmates.

HE is PROUD

He is My SON

And he will wear a bandana.

Our Creator

In awesome rainbow wonders
Breath streamed
Across the Mother earth
Turtle island.

Blessings Eagles shrieked
And thunders flapped
Their powerful wings.

Sounds of shakers
Sounds thrust forth
And *Anishinaabe* relatives
Germinated.

Water nourished suns growth
Love endurance faith
Grasps, ripens, bestowed
Fully flourished
Sculptured the ultimate given.

Migizikwe

Collected Artifacts

GRANDFATHER, THE CREATOR

My heart throbs with hurt
to see how the white brother
has crawled and bought
the Grandfather's drum and pipe.
He waited and knew
by selling him firewater
he collected artifacts.

The spirit you gave, the
prayers for the Redman, rekindle;
and younger brother, younger sisters,
cousins of all nations share the spirit.

Hopeless is in the past for it
is time when the thunderbirds
bring messages and the winds
of four directions and Mother Earth
quivers with earthquakes.

Past Grandparents were afraid of
strange white brother for they
called red brother friend, but
stripped and assimilated while pride
left and missionaries protectors
didn't understand. You gave us spirit
to care for OUR MOTHER EARTH and
all relatives.

Grandfather, Eagles carry the prayers
and Sundancers' dance, the drum of our
ancestors hasn't left.
White brother, the artifacts don't belong
to you, giver your heart peace and return
to the Redman his LIFE.

Migizikwe

For Mother

Mother,

The rays of sunlight enter and brighten
the cycle of one sun and one moon.

Mother,

The wind's breeze touches me with
your caress and I know your heart
of warmth is with me.

Mother,

I've touched the Earth, vibration of spirit, and
fluttering of Eagles direct and I
know you are with me.

Mother,

The water pounds, pulsing canals of
shimmering waves give quench. Love reveals
and heals hard times by your eyes.

Mother,

The pathways I have taken and returned home,
the Earth has awakened, hard times and tobacco
aid my understanding.

Mother,

The comfort is unseen, patience awaits.
The circle of Motherhood is blessed.

Love,
Your Daughter

Between the Nodes

Fluid web of her own creation
hearing rhythm of the heart's blood
mystic concentration of her being.

Fading of a dream
Living connective tissues
blank and expressionless features
VEILED
surfaced from dark water,
mad surreal whirl world.

The great eye reigns
a flame with nobility and courage;
leavening kind of anguish
noiseless tread and plaintive wail.

Gradually erecting the scaffolding of a nation
leap imperious truth
pulled back to its immediacy
utmost privacy.
Perplexed, dissolve fear
collapsing controlled
throbbed with nostalgia regret and repentance.
     Interlude   Entwine   Staccato
And   she   danced   between the nodes.

Message from Mother

SOUNDS
… like feathers fanning
… like a shaker
… like death rattle
… like wing flutters
something, someone, making
fluttering in the ceiling …

3 a.m.: Mother woke me up, and she wanted to give this message…
I said some prayers and listened.
Okay, Mother, what do you want me to do?

My dearly loving children
I'm thankful to each of you
for the love and support in my
final earth hours.
I'm happy and guess what?
I can be wherever I want to be.
I'll be with you in spirit.
Don't be afraid, as I'm not far …
Chances are daily life thought.
Although some of you haven't seen
or talked with me a lot. I often
thought of you each and prayed
for you especially and your children.
And I will continue to do so.

I want each of you to
continue your life to the
fullest. Treat yourself good,
and stay healthy. As you see what
abuse to your body can do.
I carried my cross in the
final hours. Thank each of
you for being there in weariness
children and grandchildren.
Take good care of your babies
and I love each of
you equally.
By the way, Thanks for the prayers.
Love, Mother
P.S.
You have fulfilled God Blessing of Honoring
your mother. Thank you and God Blessing.

November 11, 1994

In the Second Beyond Stillness

Look past the gazing *Anishinaabe* people
And into the crying of the white man.
See, they aren't happy with their way of life…
falling
below their means
…watching the government
Fly a red, white, and blue flag.
…In the name God we trust   JESUS.
…my uncle said, our people never would
Crucify a spiritual leader.
…Forgiveness, setting the proper flight of prayer
Adding more medicine water to the rock…
…in the second beyond stillness.

Pronounced: a-ni-shi-NA-bae, means those tribes now known as Ottawa, Potawatomi, and Ojibwe.

DANCE A NEW LIFE

IN THE YEAR OF 2004, I WAIT FOR GOD'S HOLY PRESENCE AS HE BLESSES.

MY PATH WILL UNFOLD IN HIS GLORIOUS LOVE

AND HIS LIGHT SHINES UPON ME.

"BLESSED ARE THEY WHO COME IN THE NAME OF THE LORD"

A BREATH OF FRESH AIR

FULFILLING THE SPIRIT WITH JOY, HAPPINESS.

FAITH NURTURES MY SPIRIT TO GO FORTH

WITH ABUNDANCE.

RICHNESS OF THE SOUL FLOURISHES, AS IT LISTENS TO THE LESSONS

WITH QUIET WISDOM.

ONE DAY AT A TIME, EACH SECOND IS SO PRECIOUS.

HARK TO THE SPIRITUAL ANGELS AS THEY PROTECT ME/US FROM

THE WORLDLY WAYS.

I DANCE A NEW LIFE.

THANK YOU, JESUS, FOR YOUR LOVE.

If I Live

If I live the way the non-Indians live, is that really me.

I must walk two paths at one time, one being the one
That I was created for to be *anishinaabe ikwe* and to
Live in the cultural life of peace. It is very special and
I honor my older relatives that prayed for us here
Today— for they knew what I would be going through.

Thank you grandmothers and grandfathers. The other
Assimilation lie is to know the requirements of the
Society, to get the education, to work in the field of
Education helping our youth. I continue to work with
Our youth at the school. It is a reward to share the
Knowledge and the language.

Aabinoojiyag   aabinoojiyak   aabinoojiyag
Laughter playing   in the hallways
On their way to another class.

BIZINDIN   AS THEY BEGIN TO LISTEN

EAGER TO LEARN AND MUCH ENERGY, THE

ONES THAT ARE READY FOR CLASS.

A TOOL

I AM the Father, the Son, the Spirit
The three trees of life.
Branches that caress vibrations,
Shadows darken the background
I stand watching and giving direction.

I AM the path of horizons,
The heartbeat.
Spiritually we're one.
Three nights, three morns, and the
Fourth fulfills offering.

I AM a tool used with harmony of
Mother, Brother and Sister.
Father, Grandma, Grandpa,
Each power in unison.

I AM the purifying season,
the life aftermath,
the new life season,
the covering quilt season.

Purify

Purify and ask the Great Spirit
He is with human spirit
On Mother Earth.

Purify and sacrifice and be humble.
He is the blessed sacred rocks
And water of the Mother Earth.

Purify with the relatives and
Pray for them. Share, be kind,
The spirit is a circle.

Purify from the sacred fire
For strengths of the three circles of
Mental, physical and spiritual.

Purify and the medicines help, *asemaa* offered,
With the pipe, cedar, sweet grass, sage
Are the strength.

Purify for the spirit journey nears.
To be red blood, to be one.
The love of the Creator is now.
Gathering with his drum.

Today My Relatives

This is your beginning. The Great Spirit
Enhances all circle in harmony.
The mystery of spirits comes from within.

Lesson and knowledge
Spread with Eagle flutters,
And the four sacred directions
Help prepare.

Today My Relative this
Is when the Grandfather Sun
And Grandmother Moon revolve,
And medicines of Mother Earth heal.

The path of our struggles has
Not lost the spirit of ancestors,
While younger generations relate.

YOU ARE!

The softness of woman, and kindness
Of manhood, sharing the sacred hoop.
It is a must to be clear of understanding,
So now my relatives, ALL are related.

Migizikwe

No Reason To Be Lost

Like the petals of a flower
Crumpled and wilted
Fallen to the earth.

How did this happen! Inside storm.

My rainbow doesn't shine in the future,
Unless my path soars with the Eagles.
He watches and sends the thunderbirds
To awaken all relatives.

Soon all relatives
Will hear Grandfather messages,
To follow his path and
Soar with the Eagle and

No reason to be LOST.

EAGLE OF THE MORNING SUNRISE

I OFFER MY *ASEMAA*
FOR MY RELATIVES
THAT THEY MAY LIVE.

LIVE FOR THIS DAY GIVEN.
TO HAVE JOY IN THEIR HEARTS,
PRECIOUS IS THE MOMENT
NOW IS FOREVER.

"GOODMORNING MY RELATIVES,"
THE BIRDS SING.
FLUTTERS FROM OUR FOUR DIRECTIONS
HARMONIZE GRATITUDE.

PINKS AND BLUES REFLECTING FROM THE SKY
ACROSS THE LAKE
I STOOD IN THE MORNING DAWN
JOYFUL.

MIGIZIKWE
AUGUST 2004

FLUTE SONG

Whey The Great Spirit

Whey,
the Great Spirit
he knows you can
feel him in the four directions,
and Mother Earth.

He knows that
Grandfather Sun and
Grandmother Moon transcend powers
to the turtle island.

Eagle man, eagle woman,
brother, sister, all relatives,
the pipe of great power
creates harmony.

rainbow colors
enlighten vast strengths
of nations, of generations.

Handle Gently

Like flowers of Mother Earth
people should and shall
be handled

gently.

Like each petal
volcanos, our limbs embrace

gently.

To toss away the
non-friendships that
exist and bring a closeness

gently.

Like the center of a flower
people shall encounter
and be handled

gently.

MY TRIP TO NEENAH

IN FEBRUARY 2009
I TRAVELLED WITH *NIIZHO'MAINGAN* TO THE WIGWAM
OF DENNIS AND CYNDI HAWK.
ARRIVING ON FRIDAY AFTERNOON.
WE HAD CHILI AND CORN BREAD. YUMMY HOT OUT OF
THE OVEN.

THERE I MET FOR THE SECOND TIME "SPOTTED HORSE"
ALSO KNOWN AS GEORGE LEDUC AGAIN WITH A KIND
GENTLE VOICE THE SAME WAY HE PLAYS THE FLUTE.
I HONORED THIS VIETNAM VETERAN WITH EAGLE
FEATHERS. HE ASKED ME SAY A PRAYER FOR HIS EAGLE
STAFF. IT SURE WAS A SIGHT TO SEE, WHEN PEOPLE
GAZE AT THEM THEY WILL FEEL THE POWER OF THE
GREAT SPIRIT GOD.
HE LIVES IN IOWA, FROM THE NATION OF THE
MI'KMAQ FIRST NATION CANADA, AYE.
HE'S CALLED TO SUNDANCE. I PRAY FOR HIM AS HE
GIVES HIMSELF FOR THE PEOPLE.

DANCE MY BROTHER   DANCE DANCE

DANCE

DANCE   THE EAGLES WHISTLE!!!!!

MIGIZIKWE
MARCH 10, 2009

NASHAKWA MAKWAKWE– BEAR WOMAN–KATHY BORGENHAGEN

At the women gathering held in Lac Courte Oreilles in Sawyer, Wisconsin. She entered the arch doorway of the long house wigwam. Dressed in a buckskin dress, her aura carrying the light of rainbows and flickering sun dog rays

Our eyes greeted each other on this gifted fine morning. Sitting we waited for direction. Then songs were sung for the sacred bundles, our sacred pipes filled.

The birds and winds surrounded us with strength. Drinking water, the river of life blood of our Mother Earth, spiritual essences of our elders listened.

Nashakwa Makwakwe spoke how she helped others with healing, claiming specifically, and a vessel transferring energy through her sacred hands, the Spirit of God guides help,
then letting the stresses: spiritual,   emotional,   physical,
                   mental   be released.

Nashkwa Makwakwe talked, her sweetness Mother of honey sitting upon Mother Earth, change of seasons. Each day is a change of inner healing.
Since this time, there were many events as we became close sisters, a bouquet of flowers, old highway of kindness driving a convertible fit for the *ogichidaakwe*, Warrior Women. Ending at the Johanna Fine Teas for lunch, Rib Mountain for pipe ceremonies, dancing at the POW wows and eating fry bread tacos at the annual Bear River POW wow in Lac du Flambeau.

She is the Bear
who strengthens like many roaring waterfalls. In every moon ceremony,

I handed her the offering of kinnickinnic red willow, *Anishinaabe* tobacco from the sacred Red Willow trees, wild rice, and fish.

Nashakwa Makwakwe is the painting of sacred hands transforming energy saying; The Father God's Spirit helping as she is the vehicle. Honor to have her pray for my healing once a month as I travel to Wausau Alternative health. Let your stresses release with calmness music, sage smudge fans the aura.

Miigwech (thank you) my Bear sister … the journeys unfold now and forever.

Migizikwe Nindizhikaaz, Nov. 7, 2017

NIIYO'GIIZHIGOOKWE–Mary Ellen Baker

The lady of dedication for sobriety of the
Anishinaabe way of living.
I watched her as she prayed to the Great Spirit
standing before the grandpa fire.
The Eagles came and flapped their blessing
with her smiling face and tender doe eyes.
She was as a grandmother, auntie and sister
to her relatives.
And she didn't take any credit due, as
she reminded us of her dedication,
that the Creator makes the moves to
show the way.
And her way of recognition for others who
helped her with suggestions.

NO TURNING BACK

Niizho Ma'iinganag

When I look into your eyes,
I can see the power of your light
And I know your love is true.
As our hearts elate we share platonic
To the spirit of our souls unite.

Our Blessings we pray for healthy fulfillment,
Wholeness, healings, respect, honor.

Sound of the rain ... enhance.
Sound of the wind ... caress.
Sound of your voice ... love.

Walking the Spiritual road one day at a time.
We shall use the medicine bundles, pipes smoked,
Sweat lodge, big drum, church.
Essence of our CREATOR'S blessings come together.
ASEMAA offering prayers. JESUS heals.
Blessings.
GICHI MANIDO, Greatest Power of Heaven and Earth.
Holding close to this promised eternal life.

My FRIEND, there is no turning back.

Migizikwe Nindizhikaaz 8/20/06–3/28/08

Madoodooswan–sweatlodge

Dedicated to Ruth Ward and relatives participating in her healing lodge.

Zhawenimin indinwemaaganag—blessing all my relatives

Nongom anamie giin Waasigiizhigookwe—today prayers for Bright Day Woman.

MINOBIMAADIZIWIN—GOOD—good living.

Odapina asema opwaagan Nimishoomis—offering tobacco pipe grandfather.

Gichi-manidoo-Great Spirit   *Bizindan indinwemaganag*—listen all relatives.

Guide in this path of light with your most holy love, in this womb as we purify.

Miigwechiwendam—be thankful for your love through our lessons.

We gain your wisdom, knowledge that atones the connection needed.

No fear shall endure our spirits as we trust in you, with faith that can move mountains.

Miigwech GICHI MANIDO—Thank you HOLY GOD GREAT SPIRIT.

Zaagi Migizikwe Nindizhikaaz—love Eagle woman who I am known as.

Waaswaagoining indoonjiba—Lac du Flambeau, Wisconsin
August 19, 2007

Refreshment To My Soul

MY SPIRIT feels happy. I am letting the peace
of the GREAT SPIRIT generate through me as
this new day approaches.

Songs of the drum brings strength to our nation.
The representatives sent and selected the ones who
Will bring forth truth of survival, the drum way.

I pray for the wonderful spiritual and sharing
of a good sober life.

May the blessings of all relatives help us as we
Walk here on our Mother Earth, and the four directions touch
your spirit in human form. Enjoy what is given.

Enjoy what is given to you.   IT IS LIFE.

Migizikwe
January 1999

ANCESTRAL WOMEN OF CREATIVE SPIRIT

For MARY BURNS, jacquard weaver
ANCESTRAL WOMEN EXHIBIT

WE ARE GREAT-GRANDMOTHERS, GRANDMOTHERS, MOTHERS, DAUGHTERS, AUNTIES *GETE ANISHINAABEKWE* LIFE GIVERS, CULTURAL BEARERS. WE are the Red women earth vessels.

We are the sounds of eagle whistles, the heartbeat healing love and the backbone of our families, and local reservation or urban communities, representatives of our states. We embellish our aura with love keeping native culture alive even through assimilation. Two paths: one living and keeping our *Anishinaabe* culture by ceremonies, pipes, sun dancing, moon dancing, water walks; The other path church, school, government, councils, committees. Both paths are the major concern for the future generations leaving their individual legacies.

The drum beat life, like the smudging cedar. How the Great Spirit Gichi Manido blesses survival from our ancestor's sources of life by hearing their prayers of the past, present and future. The *Ogichidaakwe* are the center of their homes and connectors in the tree of spiritual life. Also, the relationship with sky world, grandmother moon, grandfather sun, the circle of life with four seasons and the four directions.

Their LINEAGE direct descent from our ancestors, our clans, our names, reproduced. With the perception reality, weaving the values, women of leadership giving intricate teachings to live and help their families. We are listening for our guidance which concedes the understanding of our way of life. We are reflecting the prayers from our *Gete Anishinaabe* Grandparents years ago.

We have great humbleness for reverence to OUR GREAT SPIRIT CREATOR The awareness that we are in the Creator's presence, each moment is sacred. Capturing woven images of ancestral women brings honor by dignity. Abreast reverence, awareness does reflect many life endurances. Strong hearts filled with love and kindness from "WEAVER MARY BURNS" *MIIGWECHES*.

Migizikwe Nindizhikaaz, Migizikwe Dodem, Waaswaagoning Indoonjibaa

September 22, 2016

Happy To Be Alive

This is a saying someone might say after a big health challenge.
It brought the people and family close. And most of all the trust and
Daily faith to our CREATOR. TO offer many prayers and then to
Be very thankful.

My friend told me to take the second chance and do it better.
I strive for the invisible growth.

I sing songs to harmonize and let the spirits know I am very
Grateful for their presence. As they listen to my prayers.
Miigwech.

One time on the reservation I looked outside from the window
And in my view was a glorious eagle flying over the lodge. I
Know that the prayers will be strong for the ones in need.

Biboon is the winter word in Ojibwe. It is a season of the
Comforter. A blanket of wonderful snow. To give our Mother
Earth some rest and peace. The quietness that stretches out over
The land. It brings strength.

Down the old village road I can hear the sound of the drum
Bringing strength and healings. I sure respect the singers that
Are blessed with the songs.

Yesterday my grandchildren were at my home and they filled it with the
Sounds of living. What awesome sound of beauty and growth.
Keeping the love continuing, AWESOME GRANDCHILDREN.

MINOMANIDOIKWE–Elizabeth Vetterneck

On January 7th, 1996,
She was talking and said this powerful statement:

TREAT PEOPLE AS IF IT IS THEIR LAST DAY

This is dedicated to this woman who lives a life with the belief of JESUS.
I hear her songs and her prayers of sincerity.

MY Relatives

from the sunrise in the early morning.

it is HONORABLE to walk with you in the journey.

soooo let's be fulfilled with JOY and HAPPINESS.

as we feast together for balance under the eagle wings.

Through these minutes as the day develops into the evening

sunset dusk, and the night lingers,

impressed while our Grandmother moon shines over us.

a cycle in the four directions completes ...

SACREDNESS continues

so let's travel humble and joy

PEACE

remember all paths to the tree of live

WERE we not born equal?

AS we broke the WATER of LIFE.

October 29th, 1996
Migizikwe

EAGLE SPIRIT

You flutter LIFE

Across the auras.

Your lights

Deleting and projecting

Simultaneously the love

Of two vibrations

For one balance

Migizikwe 9-7-97

NOKOMIS DIBIKI GIIZIS – GRANDMOTHER MOON

NOKOMIS DIBIKI GIIZIS YOU are LIGHT of the NIGHT.

NOKOMIS DIBIKI GIIZIS Brightly Shining FULLNESS.

GICHI MANIDO CREATOR GREAT SPIRIT SET YOU IN THE HEAVENLY SKY.

TO HELP WITH BALANCING TIDES HERE ON MOTHER EARTH.

NOKOMIS DIBIKI GIIZIS EACH MONTH WOMEN CEREMONIAL CONNECT,

NOKOMIS DIBIKAA GIIZIS MOONTIME EACH QUARTER WAXES AND WANES.

NOKOMIS DIBIKAA GIIZIS YOU ARE THE LIGHT OF THE NIGHT BRIGHTLY SHINING.

NOKOMIS DIBIKAA GIIZIS I LOVE YOU and HONOR YOU STANDING BEFORE THE SACRED FIRES.

NOKOMIS DIBIKI GIIZIS HEAR MY PRAYER OFFERING *ASEMAA*, SAGE, SWEETGRASS, CEDAR.

NOKOMIS DIBIKI GIIZIS YOU ARE THE LIGHT OF THE NIGHT BRIGHTLY SHINING FULLNESS.

NOKOMIS DIBIKI GIIZIS CHI MIIGWECH,

MIGIZIKWE NINDIZHIKAAZ DODEM MIGIZI

WOMEN OFFERING FLOWERS TO *NIBI* (WATER)

WAASWAAGONING Lake of the Torches   Lac du Flambeau, Wisconsin Mother's Day weekend.
WATERWAYS WALK Started with a Sunrise ceremony at the Bear River powwow grounds.
Sacred songs sung honoring *Gichi Manido* our GREAT SPIRIT, the Four directions, Mother Earth,
Indinwemaaganag (all our relatives), a sacred fire and sacred pipes smoked.
Giganawendaamin Nibi Megwaa Bimoseyaang - we think of the water as we walk.
As part of Creation, we are called for this SPIRITUAL WATER WAYS WALK.
To bring forth LOVE, strength and teachings. A vision of Who We Are. Humble!!!!
We walk ten miles around Indian Village road, Highway 47, Simpson road, Highway D
And back on the Indian Village road. The lakes we circle are: Flambeau Lake,
Pokegama Lake, Interlocken Lake, Moss Lake, then Bear River.   Strong defense
to defend our water.   Mother's Day weekend. What a great gift as our steps
massage   with   love and prayers.
Eagle bone whistles, shakers, fire keepers ACCEPT our *asemaa* awakening the
Sacred living circle of life. Each person praying. As we are finishing the ceremony, our
life givers women carry flowers respectfully and offer their Love and Prayers, Honor,
TO THE BEAR RIVER Sharing now,   Helping each other and for generations to come
with mind, body, spiritually, mentally, physically, emotionally.
Why we are here?   We are seeds flowering as we all share. Water is Life.

NIMAKWA

NOKOMIS is shining in the sky and soon there
Is the new birth of *Makwa* and *Migizi* as they
Travel the old roads on the reservation.

Cruising down the old Bear River road they stop
at the second bridge, right in the middle. The
seconds stopped with a breathtaking view of
the river and all the fireflies danced over the
place. Would never trade this view for city life.

Let's face it as we spend time together when we
can, we both know that it will always be this
way when the moon is full.

Waiting for the next full moon.

Migizikwe
6-26-99

LOOKING OUT ACROSS THE WATER, A SPIRITUAL LINE OF WAVES

For my friend *Giizhikgookwe*, Sky Woman Marge Greene

AFTER WALKING ONE MILE, WE REST ON SOME STUMPS. THESE STUMPS ARE FREE!! MARGE GOT THEM ALONG THE SIDE OF THE HIGHWAY D ROAD. SHE SAID, "THE STUMPS ARE FREE, I JUST STOPPED MY CAR AND PUT THEM IN THE TRUNK." SHE DELIVERED THEM TO OUR FAVORITE PLACE OF REST. THERE THE EAGLES COME AND THE HUMMINGBIRDS EAT HONEY FROM THE PLANTS AND FLOWERS.

HEALING PRAYERS, TEARS OF HAPPINESS HOPE AND JOY. SEE AND FEEL THE BEAUTY THAT OUR CREATOR HAS MADE AND GAVE US THE GIFT OF LIFE. WE SIT IN SILENCE PEERING AT THE LAKE, THINKING THOUGHTS OF RELATIVES IN NEED OF PRAYERS.

WE BRING PLASTIC BAGS TO PICK UP TRASH FROM PEOPLE TOSSING OUT OF THEIR CARS. WE HAVE A VISIT OF A YOUNG FOX, BIRDS, THE BEES GETTING NECTAR FROM FLOWERS, BEAUTY.

THE SPIRITUAL FLOWING LINES GLIMMERING AND GLISTENING WAVES OF STRENGTH.

MOMENTS ARE BLESSED. WE LEAVE AND IT'S TIME TO WALK BACK, TO BREAKFAST, CHIT CHAT OF EVENTS AND FAMILIES, WORRIES, SHARING CONCERNS, SEWING AND LISTENING TO MUSIC.

THANK YOU, CREATOR, FOR OUR FRIENDSHIP.

Substantial Evidence

in the flames, fluorescent brightness
of truth enticed life inside the teepee womb.

strength of the power
dawn of healings through all-night intervals.
songs that prayed forgiveness of trespasses.

sitting upon the Mother Earth
while smoke travelled into heaven.

all around, the FATHER'S Spirit presence
lots of Eagles flutters blessed Creator's children.

he wants them to love each other
these human spirit forms preparing
to leave at his call.

the Eagle shrieked!

WOMAN

HOW tolerance is
slowly exploding and
no peaceful atmosphere
in your lodge
IS it because
your warrior consumes
plenty firewater?
IS it hard
to live with plans of
a warrior, while he plays?
IS your heartache
realizing destruction
without a care?
IS it the man you
really wanted to share
life with, drowned?
drowned in his own world
of firewater, disabled!
WOMAN
Grandfather and Grandmother
see your sad sparks
and help to ignite
life, with winds
to set you FREE
AND BE YOU!

Of the Creation

Like the singer
beating his song
on the drum.

Life passes on,
sacred winds touch all
living existence;
three Eagle Spirits,
Pipeman,
Spirit Man Guide,
Stone Man Spirit,
Stick Man Spirit,
Water Spirit,
Grandmother Moon,
Grandfather Sun.

To the sacredness
of all creation, it is given
to share the Red, Yellow,
Black and White race.

Like the singer
beating his song
on the drum.

SNOW ANGELS ON THE ICE

On Thursday January 8th, 2009. I received a phone call from my dearest friend Frank. His Voice sounded excited and he mentioned we could do something that I wanted to do a few years ago. I completely forgot about the idea but he reminded me. I did remember that I wanted to go walking on the ice at night. So we made plans to set that time.

After the Neal McCoy show January 10th. Saturday night as we went to the early show at 7:00 p.m. held at the Lake of Torches casino in Lac du Flambeau, Wisconsin. January 10th was the full moon, a glowing circle around the moon, shining so bright in the sky.

After the show Frank drove us home in his heavy Ford to my home. Right away I changed, adding warm clothes for it was cold. Brrrrrr. I then went and got my sacred prayer pipe to fill It with tobacco for a prayer, I also had my shaker to sing three songs. Frank joined me in prayer.

WOW. Up in the sky was the grandmother moon, shining so bright. She was a full moon! the rays were like a bright day. I also know that it was a special moon according to NASA. It was known as an eclipse.

After praying I took the sacred pipe inside and laid it on the kitchen table. Then we started our trek. Walking down the small slope to the ice. It was a cold crisp night in northern Wisconsin. The crunching walkway was slightly packed down from former steps made by my grandson *Gibwanzi* (Hawk). But we were determined to reawake my idea as we walked in the deep snow, 12 inches through. On the way down, Frank picked me a walking stick that was already standing by the oak tree. Yes, it did help my balance. I felt like Moses clearing the way. I smiled inside, snow instead of water. Once we got on the lake, the depth was four to six inches on the ice.

"How far do you want to walk?" I asked. "Well as far as you want to" was Frank's reply. We walked on some more, I stopped and looked at the moon and let out a yelp, a sharp shrill cry, sort of a whoop. Making this sound with glee and joy when something is good. Aye.

We listened and we heard a yap sound of dogs barking on the north end of the lake. I wanted Frank to make a wolf sound. Because his name is *Niizho Ma'iingan*, it means Two Wolves. The moon circle formed by the light was incredible. The moonlight glistened. The snow on the ice formed sparkles like diamonds. The snow was fresh, clear, undisturbed snow. But now fresh with footprints. I said "Let's make some snow angels." Frank said, "you first." So down I went and made my snow angel. He helped me up and then he made his, then I helped him up. I wished I would have brought my camera to take a picture. I will have to come back. We laughed together. Who would think that sixty-two-year-olds would be out on the lake making snow angels? We hiked back and I filled my desire of some years ago.

It Is Well With My Soul

Morning Prayer outside of Leonardo Hotel
Be'er Sheva, Israel
May 29, 2010

Thank You, Lord, for allowing me to be here in your Holy Land! Grace be to me and others.

Grace to me and to others
Grace to me and to others
Praise to You, oh Lord, King of Kings
Honor, I say, Father in heaven
Glory to You, Lord ... glory to You, Lord.

May You bless this day upon me
With Your Love, Joy, Happiness, Health, Wealth
I sit and enjoy the uplifting Winds
Brush the earth. In quiet communion
And wait upon the Lord. A stillness enwreathes my soul.
A bird sounding fulfillments, promising the day
Enriched saying, My Lord, My Lord
Miigwechwenima (Thank You) Father God.
Give me this day my daily bread.
Another bird confirms: Spirit, Spirit, Spirit.

Thank you, Lord for my health, for my Companions,
My Children, my Grandchildren, Relatives, Sisters, Brothers,
Friends and all my Aglow Relatives.

Standing is Sacredness today
As I walk upon the earth.
Come to His Tree of Life. Amen.

Praises to You, Father God, Jesus, Holy Spirit.

FOR THE *ANISHINAABE* PEOPLE

crazy crane
long braids   stood remembering . . .

the teachings of the ELDERS,
that have already gone to the spirit world.

before the white man came,
how close of a relationship they had with *GIZHE MANIDO*.
the close spiritual love.

nowadays,
tsometime in the past the rejected white people
came to our Mother Earth Turtle Island
because
they were supposed to learn from the REDMAN
how to be reverent and to respect and be
THANKFUL for what has been given.

OH, when will they learn . . .
and then he thought . . . of JESUS and the
TEN COMMANDMENTS he gave them to live by.

OH, when will they learn . . .

Nowadays,
GOD gave his laws. GOD also gave to the REDMAN the
blessings of the Native American Church. He knew
GOD'S pity for them.

The Indian had to forgive, the people who want to hurt them.
the ones who defy his law.
the ones who don't believe in JESUS.
the ones who don't believe our treaty rights and the
constitution of the United States, for without respect
of the treaties, neither is the United States constitution respected.

OH, How Are They Ever Going To Learn . . .

1-19-85

For Lac du Flambeau Relatives

crazy crane
stood by sand beach peering across the shimmering water
toward medicine rock...he glanced at strawberry island
the last war with the Sioux.

the waves splitting his Indian image, yellow water lilies ballade
lips silently invocate: an Eagle's ululating shriek brought his vision.

into the mist, like a Washington man the historical
anachronism that parched and trampled...blurs of big brother
Indian programs, HUD, tourism, alcoholism...he was
seeing through the wary eye...suffering bizarre insults,
parade of personalities of economic, political, religion
that confiscated homeland and freedom...pills for
schizophrenia memoir

bubbles of sweat...

it matched the rain pouring down, while the thunderbirds
set the pattern overture...hard tears...the earth...
quietly his feet wiggled in the muck....

he was not crazy   HE didn't want.

9-24-82

THE BUS RIDE

In the year of 1965, I lived at 540 North Street in Milwaukee, Wisconsin. It is one block south of Wisconsin Avenue. Well, I worked at Western hardware on the east side. So my way of getting to work was to catch the bus. My route was Wisconsin Avenue to Humboldt Street on the east side to transfer north.

So one morning I was running a little late, I grabbed my trench coat out of the closet and took off literally running to get the 6:30 a.m. bus. I was really running up the slope to the avenue. Aha, I just made the bus … "Whew!" Cheered by the thought I wouldn't be late for work, looking out the window, I got closer to my stop and stood up to pull the cord so the bus driver knew it was my destination at the next bus stop.

Standing outside at the bus exchange, I stood attentively looking for the next bus. Suddenly a man voice said, "Mama, do you know you have a coat hanger hanging on the ties of your coat? I replied, "Yes, I always carry my hanger with me. Thank YOU."
At that moment I inwardly was busting a gut laugh, keeping myself intact not to laugh out loud. The bus stopped and I walked up the steps smiling, a big happy smile.

WALK TO THE WOODSTOVE

The daily routine in the morning around 7:00 to 7:45. I put on some warm clothes; a jacket Frank gives me with snap-up buttons, my Packers pants, my wool socks, boots, my red hat with attached scarf. I will be warm. Oh, I need to bring my *asemaa* (tobacco) along to offer in the fire. Okay, my dog Lovey is ready too, she is excited, wagging her tail, jumping around. I open the door and here we go. We walk the trail which is slightly bumpy due to the fact that when I had the roof shoveled, it piled it up. I had to make another trail over the old one. I walk gingerly on the crunchy snow, I like the sound the snow makes. Oh Jesus, help me so I won't fall. Lovey runs ahead to do her routine down the hill looking for her squirrel that she thinks she can catch. Also there is a rabbit there, as I see the rabbit footprints that circle the house each day. That rabbit must be up really early. Although one morning she came running up the hill and stopped short as she saw me standing there and looked at me, then bounced on a run. What a beautiful rabbit! There is a saying, you see a rabbit you have good luck. I smiled. I do need lots of luck, the lottery, bingo, to mention a few.

I reach the woodshed made from the carport I bought this year, I don't know why I didn't think of it before. Frank put boards on three sides to keep the snow out, it really looks like a woodshed now. On the ground Frank put pallets to keep the wood off the ground, what an amazing idea. I was proud we had a new woodshed.

I feel sad my wood stack is almost gone, I estimated four or five more times to fill the stove counting the evening fill. But spring is near, we just had daylight savings time change, Spring ahead March 8th.

I love the walk to the wood stove, it gives me exercise, breath of fresh cold Wisconsin air. I like to see the sunrise come up and meditate on the prayers for my children, grandchildren, Frank and others I know in need of some good thoughts. Well I walk back to the house, the stove will be good until the evening fill, now my house will be cozy all day.

Migizikwe   March 9, 2009

ISHKODE

Ishkode grew up on an Indian reservation.
He was very handsome with emerald green eyes
and black coal hair. He had a warm heart,
he loved doing good things for the people.
Some of the elders said, "He was a blessing from
Gichi Manido our Great Spirit Creator God."
But *Ishkode* didn't know he was blessed yet.

Then something happened to him one day as he was becoming a young warrior. He was out walking amongst the trees and animals of the forest.

"HEY *ISHKODE*, Look up into the sky and watch the clouds." Ishkode looked around to see who was speaking to him. Gosh, he thought. At first he looked on the ground and a little ant looked him square in the eye.

Ishkode said, "Little red ant, why do you want me to look up at the sky and watch the clouds?"

Ant said, "Because *Gichi Manido* Great Spirit wants you to seek guidance and a message that will be given to you."

Here *Ishkode* then stood up very attentively. He didn't move a muscle. Respectfully an aura of light surrounded the area. *Ishkode*'s eyes searched the clouds. They glowed luminous and revealed a path of life.

Astonished! *Ishkode* knew what he must do.

For Priority

our pathways divide.
there beyond the horizon
awaits my travel,
another journey, big iron horse.
I look into the future . . .

while I'm gone the Eagle protects.
let the Morning Star bless your day
let the Sun shine the peacefulness
let the Four Winds caress your spirit
let the Grandma Moon flow internal water,
Purifying your strength.
while I'm gone the Eagle protects.
let the Great Spirit hear your voice
singing ancestors songs.
angels, spirit guides talking,
winds of the mountains.
walk softly in moccasins, blessed are
they in flight to the tree of life.
these prayers bring crystal clear love.

Dedicated to Steve Bowman, Navajo
Sanostee, New Mexico

Looking into the Sun

A little farther down the road
from Crowdog's paradise
is this place known as
Ghost Hawk Park.
People would go there to
swim and wash up.
One evening I went over there
with Floyd Redcrow Westerman,
we sat there and visited.
I seen his spirit.
Spirit of grandfather,
older with silver gray hair.
Forever young he was at
the time.
Being the ole man, he travels
with messages of Eagle flights.
As we danced, everyone prayed
Sundance sacrifice, we have been
called to the tree of life.
I like his song, Going Back.
We were picking up the
pieces left for us.
Our grandparents knew we would
enjoy our traditions.
Looking into the sun.
For Floyd Westerman

VISIONS OF MEMORIES

Building a relationship, walking through the woods, swimming in the water,

exercise, exercise.

Riding in a car under the stars, jogging over sand and rocks.

Butterfly flutters, Hawk is blessing the grounds, Eagle circles above.

Treaty rights, the Chippewa nation hunters wear blaze orange

Hunting for deer, ducks, wild rice harvest,

Canoe to medicine rock, then later sit in a sweat lodge

Praying with the sacred pipe,

The road, the path of endurance,

Hand and hand, hand and hand, prayer and prayer, prayer and prayer,

building relationships, thanking our ancestors.

Sweat Lodge

She remembered the sweat lodges,
she remembered . . .

Cedar fulfilling,
giving a clearance of
purity.

Each person came for a purpose,
a main purpose
and individual needs
to talk, pray
to the Great Spirit.

a warm smile silently inside
filled her heart,
even though some people
she didn't know,
already felt a kinship.

Older Eagle

The human healer
Older Eagle looked into young Eagle eyes
and spoke of the journey
Heal

He strengthens the spine and
sings songs
don't forget me, Older Eagle –
I can grow to more than flutters.

Put the blessings in your bundle
talons to grasp the golden light
the light of truth
salvation

Our greatest highest Spirit
looking down to see the
enlightenment of creation
Heal Heal Heal Heal

We Are One

We Are One

A cycle with Grandfather Sun
and Grandmother Moon.
Our sister Morning Star
and Brother Evening Star.

We Are One

With the four winds touching
and the tree relatives give us breath.
Mother Earth provides live in our struggle.

We Are One

Each sacred morning, the Eagle awakes
with guidance, blessing as he protects.

We Are One

Hearing our Grandfathers drum,
giving the culture. In this contemporary era.
Together we shall travel in harmony.

NIIWIN GAKEYAA

GIIWEDINONG – NORTH *WAABINONG* – EAST
ZHAAWANONG – SOUTH *NINGAABIIANONG* – WEST

FOUR RACES

ANISHINAABEG – RED   *WAABISHKIWEJIIG* – WHITE

ANIBIISHAABOO BIMAADIZIIJIG – YELLOW

MAKADE WIIYAAS – BLACK

WAASAMOWAG ANIMIKIIG – Lightning flashing.

MADWEWED A'AW DEWE'IGAN – Sound that drum.

MII'OMAA WENJI BAAMAGAK BIMAADIZIWIN – That is where life comes from.

GAKINA BIMAADIZIJIJIG – All living beings.

DISBISHKOO WAAWIIYEYAG – Like the circle (of life).

OZAAWABIK   *MIGIZIKWE*
Elder Joe Chosa   Elder Mildred Tinker Schuman

NIIBIN 2010

Dear

Today I looked into my spirit.
Searching for the gift of Spiritual blessings.
I was thankful to be what and who I am
Continually searching, seeking the Creator.
The spiritual balances of life, I am thankful that I
could pray to the Creator.
Light the pipe of peace,
Woman Staff
Cedar, Sage, Sweet grass,
Everlasting strength…

I am content. *Miigwech*.

April 6, 1989

MINO BIMAADIZIWIN

GOOD LIVING: I THOUGHT OF WHAT THIS WOULD MEAN? AND APPLY IT TO MY DAILY LIVING.
AND HERE ARE SOME OF MY OWN THOUGHTS:
EACH DAY I AM VERY THANKFUL TO BE HERE ON OUR SACRED MOTHER EARTH, I SAY *MIIGWECHES* TO OUR GREAT SPIRIT FOR THIS LIFE. ONE DAY AT A TIME I LIVE.
I APPRECIATE
WHAT GIFTS I HAVE. MY CHILDREN, MY GRANDCHILDREN, GREAT GRANDCHILDREN, MY SPIRITUAL CHILDREN, MY RELATIVES. I HAVE LOTS OF SPIRITUAL RELATIVES THAT ARE LIVING A GOOD LIFE. BY THIS GOOD LIFE, THEY GO TO CEREMONIES OR OTHER CHURCHES. LIVING FREE FROM ALCOHOL AND OTHER DRUGS. GETTING TO KNOW SELF. SELF RELATES TO YOUR FEELING, YOUR SPIRITUAL BELIEFS, YOUR EMOTIONAL FEELINGS, WHAT YOU'RE THINKING IS THE MENTAL FEELINGS, AND YOUR PHYSICAL PATH OF LIFE, TAKING CARE TO EXERCISE AND KEEP THE BODY HEALTHY.
CHANGE: SOMETIMES WE HAVE TO CHANGE A LOT OF DIFFERENT THINGS IN OUR LIVES: HOW? WHY? OUTCOME? PLANS?
PART OF THE CHANGE IS TO HAVE RESPECT FOR SELF AND FOR OTHERS. NO MATTER WHAT THAT PERSON IS LIKE, THAT'S THE WAY THEY ARE AND WE MUST RESPECT THE OTHER, THIS IS CALLED UNCONDITIONAL LOVE.
LET US SHARE THE GIFT OF LIFE OUR GREAT SPIRIT GAVE US, AND LET'S BE THANKFUL FOR IT AND STAY CLOSE TO HIM.
LOVE AND PRAYERS TO YOU, *MIGIZIKWE*   May 8, 1997

Precious You

from the seed of life
there is precious you
to be thankful for.

you consist
existing body:

precious for its physical being
precious for its mental being
precious for its spiritual being

it is realized
interference of jagged waves
splash corrupted vibes.

precious, the Creator controls
trust and faith of yourself,
you are not alone.

Early Morning

Here it is
The breaking of dawn
Looking out the window
Across the lake I see the new light.
In this fall season, a blue crimson pale skyline blesses.

I ponder the many projects needing to be done.
I perceive the first need.
Not to get caught up in the busyness of many.
Free with the freshness of the new day.

HONORS to the GREAT SPIRIT
I breathe as I go outside on the lawn and raise my arms upward.
For the promise of the new life today,
Offering my prayers of thankfulness,
Giving my tobacco by the cedar tree for my family,
Relatives and friends.

I am joyful!!!!

Big Reservation in the Sky

Gichi Ishkoniganing Giizhigong
Dedicated to Bill Sutton

Imaa Nimbimoseyaan akiingingiinoodawaa binesii ganozhid.
as I walk upon the earth I heard the Eagle call my name.

Ikido Gichi Manido danaziikonan.
He said, the Great Spirit sent me to you.

Giiwii ayaawig dabii izhaayaan omitigobimaadiziiwin.
He wants you to come to his tree of life.

Ayaamagad ayaawin ishpiming iwidi Gitchi Manido ayaad.
There's a place beyond the earth where the Great Spirit dwells.

Indizhaa iwidi ishkoniging.
I am going to that big reservation

binesii ooniingwiiganaang inganiiaya.
going under the Eagle wings.

Gizaagii'ig miinawaa gimiinig izhaawin.
He loves you and gives you guidance

Minawaa giiganawenimig miinawaa gidanii ganawabamig.
and protection and security.

Geget niwiizhaa-iwidii gitchi ishkoniganing
Yes, I am going to the Big Reservation

Binesii o'oniigwiiganaang inganiiayaa
going under the Eagle wings

gichi ishkoniganing giizhigoong
Big Reservation in the sky.

ABOUT THE AUTHOR

Mildred "Tinker" Schuman is a free verse published poet, storyteller, and spiritual helper. She is a member of the Ojibwe Nation of Lac du Flambeau, Wisconsin. Her Native name is *Migizikwe*, or Eagle Woman.

Tinker attended the Institute of American Indian Arts in Santa Fe, New Mexico, and has a Bachelor of Arts degree in Education and Creative Writing.

As a poet, her work is established in Native American heritage, but is related and relevant to all walks of life, the pathways of travel on Mother Earth. She is the author of a trilogy entitled *Reflections*, with the first volume titled *Reborn in the Sun*. She is also the co-author of *The Healing Blanket* and a poetry CD *All My Relatives: Gakina Nin De Was Maa*.

Tinker says about her work: "Expression of Life through my art, whether poetry, painting, drawing, beadwork, writing short stories, dancing, singing these phrases of my experiences, my life beliefs, my spiritual life…that is native tradition."

Her many accolades include being presented with the "Elder of the Year Award" by the Wisconsin Indian Education Association. She was also featured in Mary Burns' "Ancestral Women" weaving exhibit.

Tinker continues to share her artistic compilations through dancing, singing, writing and visual arts.

www.ingramcontent.com/pod-product-compliance
Lightning Source LLC
Chambersburg PA
CBHW082337300426
44109CB00045B/2457